Poetry Fr...

regarding Pathways ...

words of love and sharing -

thoughts and feelings
memories and dreams
special days, special people

words of caring and repairing -

whether in rhyme or free versity
the messages reveal great diversity

wondrous events - beyond measure
insights for all to treasure

It's an honor to preview and edit
this opus -
and bow to the author - who earns
all the credit.

So let's join hands
and sing her praises
Let the whole world know it
Laurel Freeman, is indeed
A most distinguished poet!

Doris Bardon has published several books, **Yes You Can II***, and* **Museums and More.**
*She is very active in the Gainesville community, with the arts and has
written for several mazagines and newsletters. It is an honor to share
this poem as it brings a smile to my eyes.*

Doris Bardon© 9/9/99

To Janene,
May all your
path take you
on a wonderful
journey ♡ ♡
♡ Laurel ♡
12/10/99

Pathways

on a

Journey

by

Laurel J. Freeman

Published by:
Freeman USA, Inc.
2622 NW 43rd Street, Suite C1
Gainesville, FL 32606
(352) 371-9689

First Edition

Printed by Special Publications Inc.
743 S.E. Fort King Street
Ocala, Florida 34471

The picture on the front cover was taken by
Audrey W. Hammond of London, England.
It is of the garden, at the home of
Claude Monet at Giverny, France.
Picture was computer enhanced by
Kevin Fortin and Ian Phillips of Gainesville, Florida.

Published by:
Freeman USA, Inc.
2622 NW 43rd Street, Suite C1
Gainesville, FL 32606
(352) 371-9689

I wish to dedicate

Pathways on a Journey

to:

The love of people

The love of oneness

The love of life

The love of communication

The love of all

Peace on Earth

Table of Contents

Acknowledgments

Pathways on a Journey has been just that, a journey with many paths. This book was made possible because of the synergy of many.

With love I thank the following people:

♥ Breezy Freeman, my Mom, who gave me the opportunity to be creative and taught me to be responsible for all my actions. I love her for those qualities.

♥ Morris Kaufmann, my Dad, who left when I was five and by leaving showed me a path that helped shaped me into who I am today.

> Some of the paths I have choosen are because of my parents. I honor and love them for who they are and what they brought into my life's journey.

♥ Howard Freeman, my beloved husband, for supporting me on many levels as I walk my journey toward my highest self.

♥ Carolyne Freeman, our daughter, for her wisdom, being present in every way and for challenging me to strive to be a better mother and friend.

♥ Bonnie Freeman, our daughter, who while she walked her path on Earth was an example for living and staying in the present.

♥ Doris Bardon, a friend and relative, whose energy is phenomenal and a continual reminder to "go for it."

💜 Amber Waters, a friend, who challenges me in positive ways.

💜 Mom, Dad, Doris Cousin, Uncle Sam Goldstein and Michael Swanson for taking their time for editing and seeing all the "i's" are dotted and the "t's" are crossed.

💜 All my family, friends, and clients who gave me feedback, great material, and who care.

💜 All the family and friends who chose to share their thoughts with others in the Chapter "Bridging Pathways".

💜 My staff, Lelaine, Vanessa, 3 Kelly's, Erika, Megan and 2 Michael's, who have helped type in poems, finish the layout and wrap up things.

💜 Michelle Runyon for starting the publication process.

💜 Audrey W. Hammond from London, England who took the picture for the front cover.

💜 Kevin Fortin and Ian Phillips for the computer enhanced front cover.

💜 Special Publications, Inc., the printing company for delivering a finished product.

💜 You, the reader for the joy of sharing.

With 💜 and 💡 To Your Health,
💜

Laurel

COMINGS

and

GOINGS

Chapter Introduction

Comings and Goings is about our own journey. We all choose different paths to explore. Each path we choose is a learning experience. If we choose, each learning experience allows us to move to another path. We have the opportunity for many choices.

Many of us are coming and going at the same time. We are moving toward or away from different thought processes and experiences.

Each journey is about life and thoughts. Depending on time, space and awareness is how we view the past, future and present of our own coming and going. Or maybe, our view of our past, present, and future comings and goings is dependent on time, space and our awareness.

These thoughts and poems are a collection of my awareness of my comings and goings in life. Since I am responsible for all of my thoughts and actions, my main goal in life is to move toward my highest self. I believe in being as respectful to others as I would be to myself.

It is my honor and privilege to know many people from many communities and walks of life. As our paths cross or move along the same avenues, we interact with each other and each situation or experience. We may choose to embrace those encounters as we are all coming and going. ♥

Laurel J. Freeman© 7/26/99

The 2 of Us

Leaving Bar Harbor
Is quite a sight.
First stop to fill up
And then "hit the road".

With our panoramic view
And the skies so blue
It's easy to review
All our activities
Of the past week.

Now driving down Route 3
Each in silent thought,
Just the 2 of us.

The designated driver
Alert and watching the road
With postcard scenery passing by.

The official map reader
Drifts off to a gentle slumber
Leaving the driver to thought;
And to wonder.

Solo on this rolling route,
Another car then joins
To share the splendor;
Now, there are 2 of us.

What is that driver thinking
In the car ahead?
Are his thoughts on
The wonderment before his eyes?
Or only with getting to his job,
Or to home?

Not taking a minute
To enjoy and to breathe,
The fresh sea air
Through windows open wide,
Oh! yes,
A blend in perfect balance;
Allowing the sweetest aroma
That only nature can.

Just the 2 of us,
Winding over hill and dale.
Dotted with homes throughout.
Some are large and
Seem to expand as their owners
Added a garage here,
Barn and porches there.
Just the 2 of us,
Seeing a cemetery
Beside a row of houses.
I wondered,
Where were all these people from?

Laurel J. Freeman© 8/23/90

What were they like
The ones that came to live
And to die here?
Who lay buried in those orderly rows?
Each marked with headstone
How could there be so many?
Or are they combined to
Hundreds of years?

Just the 2 of us,
Passing lakes of
Rich blues and
Pines of ever so green.
The mountains ahead
With little patches
Sparsely put here and there,
For crops to grow
So green and lush.

Just the 2 of us,
See those cabins in a row,
And sailboats swaying
To gently lapping waters.

Then in rhythmic motion
As if to say
There is no other time
Or place
It is only
Now,
That counts.

Just the 2 of us,
As we round the bend
With little bridges,
Linking, yet another town.

Ellsworth, Rockport,
Seal Harbor, Belfast

Just the 2 of us,
He turns,
Leaving for his designated destination.

Simultaneously,
The official map reader
Opens his eyes,
Stretches and wakens.
Route 3 continues to Augusta,
with
Just the 2 of us. ❤

Returning from Maine.
Laurel J. Freeman© 8/23/90

The Visit

I'd just love to stay in bed and visit with my head;
However, I have things to do.

To recite, consider and ponder,
Oh, what a treat to let my mind wonder;
However, I have things to do.

Some days are made to snuggle up,
Have breakfast in bed with a large coffee cup;
However, I have things to do.

World peace, education and thoughts like that,
Are waiting to be solved, when lying still on a mat;
However, I have things to do.

If I lie real still, with covers drawn,
I may not move 'till another dawn;
However, I have things to do.

A thought of that and a thought of this,
Oh, to stay in bed just once seems bliss;
However, I have things to do.

And if I close my eyes to meditate,
I will transport myself into another state;
However, I have things to do.

Oh, jeepers, I have got to get going,
Do laundry, dishes, straightening and mowing;
How well I know there are things to do.

Oh, but once
To stay in bed and visit with my head would be fun;
Especially knowing
Everything always seems to get done.❤

Laurel J. Freeman© 12/22/93

The Wheel

Spin and weave the medicine wheel,
Through the years of time.
Adding knowledge to be shared with all,
Increasing harmony and peace.
Expanding love and truth of the oneness,
We are encircled in the wheel.
Ever moving,
Up and down,
All around,
With no beginning,
With no end. ❤

Laurel J. Freeman© 7/18/93

Moon Dances

On our early morning walk one day,
We had a surprise when the Moon turned our way.
The Moon was dancing across the sky,
As Venus held it up from a string above,
Three inches at most was that string
As the sliver of Moon beaming down on us
Was dancing across the sky, as easy as could be.
Just for Howard and me to see.
The Star shone so brightly and so did the Moon.
As a fresh picture painted.
The Moon dances.
Days later we took a short walk at night,
In time to see the full Moon dancing
with the trees in its light.
The clouds cleverly made
pictures in the sky;
Like a dog gobbling up the Moon which was near by.
Then the Moon appeared again, dancing;
The Moon and the Sky.
The trees moved and swayed to the gentle breeze,
As the Moon danced and played
in-between the branches.
In timeless fun and constant glow,
The Moon dances each night
while it orbits our small planet
Bringing light and all the playful magic.
During the day or the night,
The Moon glows
As the Moon dances. ❤

Laurel J. Freeman© 2/27/95

Thanks

The morning star shines brightly,
Joyfully the day awakens.
Another path to journey,
Choices to choose,
I give thanks.

Our choices to be our own,
As our paths wind,
spiraling ever upward
toward the Sun.
Each in our own dance.
I give thanks.

Sometimes we stop,
As if the Earth stood still,
To ask,
Is this the right choice?
We ask ourselves and others;
Knowing,
We are all in this together.
I give thanks.

Our path is our own,
Our journey shared.
Each path on our journey,
Brings us to where we are going.
I give thanks.

Laurel J. Freeman© 11/28/96

Our souls touch on many levels,
Our hearts intertwine in love.
Opening,
Expanding the true
Spirit of oneness,
Encompassing all.
I give thanks.

May each day be fulfilled.
The knowledge of knowing,
The essence of being,
The idea of thinking,
The opportunity to create,
The path is ours to choose.
I give thanks.

The sun dances high above our small planet,
As it, too, is on a path.
We move and turn,
As Jupiter holds up the Moon,
Shining as brightly as the morning star.
A day of choices,
Past.

I give thanks. ❤

Laurel J. Freeman© 11/28/96

Thoughts of Love and Life

When seeing

                    the light

and then

        being the light

                one

                            becomes
the light

        and you are

                light. ❤

Laurel J. Freeman© 6/8/97

Chanting on the Mountain

Oh, great spirit of the mountain,
Life force in every divine manifestation.

Oh, great spirit of the mountain,
Grant fire deep within.

Oh, great spirit of the mountain,
Dance among the trees.

Oh, great spirit of the mountain,
Move waters to allow the new.

Oh, great spirit of the mountain,
Grow plants for those in need.

Oh, great spirit of the mountain,
Bring harmony to the children.

Oh, great spirit of the mountain,
Help them open their hearts to know.

Oh, great spirit of the mountain.❤

Coming back from a hike in Glacier National Forest.

Laurel J. Freeman© 8/4/96

Thoughts

Why do
the words
come
flowing,
rolling
and
tossing,
when there
is
no time,
no paper?

These
thoughts
lost
in the
mind
forever. ❤

Laurel J. Freeman© 1/10/95

Balance

There is balance as I call upon the spirits of the planet.
The North Winds stir the thoughts of consciousness,
The South Winds bring awareness,
As West Winds surrender to love,
While East Winds are adorned with caring.
Winds from above circle in swirls of yangs,
From far below the surface are winds of yings,
Winding their way to the opening.

Hear softly the drummer beat to the sounds of the heart,
Stop to listen as the cry of compassion awakens,
For the world has been standing,
Sleeping on its feet.
Arise as the drum beats,
Joining to increase the visions of peace.
Drum to the Winds,
Move to the drums,
Winds move the drums,
Each dancing to the joy of life.
Give thanks for balance the universe brings,
Give thanks for uniting the threads of time,
Which link us into one.

For one is balance,
For one hears the pulse of all,
For one can not go alone,
For all join together to create,
One,
In harmony and balance. ❤

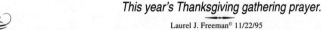
This year's Thanksgiving gathering prayer.
Laurel J. Freeman© 11/22/95

Out

I see the morning dew,
The vapors from the fog
Surrounding what is near
All before the sun begins to rise.
The clean, moistened air fills one's nostrils
To contentment.
Out, out on a morning hunt.
The doe delicately dances across the field.
The buck is not large enough.
The ducks are ready to flush,
Some still waking
To the coming dawn.
The wild turkeys moving, calling,
Letting everyone know it is time.
Time, time to be out on a morning hunt. ❤

Going Home

Going home.

To remember the days of those young years,
with all the hopes and all the fears.
To remember
the play and
hard, hard work
of growing up.
Then, the moving on.

Going home.

Time to pause, to catch my breath,
to think of going home.
To look upon a street so big,
somehow it grew so small.
All the remembered happenings
seemed so endless and now confused.

How could everything diminish in every way
and yet,
the big seem big?

Then, the moving on. ❤

Returning to Pocatello, Idaho was an incredible experience. It seemed
so many years ago and like yesterday wrapped into one moment of time. As a child,
everything was immense and endless. As an adult everything is
diminutive and fleeting. I always wondered where the saying
"Making mountains out of mole hills" came from and what it means. Now I know.

Laurel J. Freeman© 8/14/95

Child Thoughts

I remember we were looking for a house to buy. My parents wanted to be near the college for convenience. We came into a neighborhood where all the streets were named for well known universities. I thought it funny, being only five and not even sure what a college was. We drove down Stanford Street. On the lawn of the house for sale was our dog, Star, walking across the lawn.

Star had been missing for days. He did not fancy being tied up on a very short rope, since we were staying in a small, ugly, dingy motel.

Well, you might imagine the reunion. We were so excited to see Star, we almost forgot to look at the house. Of course, my mother saw it as a sign.

This was the house for her, and Star had picked it out. So that was that, it must be the right home.

My mother believed Star was her father reincarnated. He was her protector and adviser, and he never talked back. He gave unconditional love.

Shortly, after the reunion, we moved to 87 Stanford Street, the third house in a cul-de-sac. The open fields were our playgrounds; a big red clay mountain was the best to climb.

On the other side of the mountain was the "I" carved out above the stadium. It stood for Idaho State College. A great place to sit and to watch a football game, even if I didn't understand one thing about it. I did like to hear the band and to watch all the people come and go.

In the summer, the stadium was used as a drive-in theatre. We would sit on the stadium seats instead of in cars. We would bring our blankets and snacks and watch movies like "My Friend Flicka" and "Snowfire". That year was when I decided to marry a horse.

One summer my grandmother, our Nana, came and bought me a bike, which became my horse. I had learned to ride a bike with no brakes. After the big bike wreck, I guess Nana felt I should have a bike with brakes.

I would ride like the wind, always careful to ride around the ants. I always thought ants had special powers and never wanted to hurt any of them. Have you ever tried to ride around an ant pile without killing any of them? It is quite a trick. ❤

Revisiting the home I grew up in evoked many memories. Nana never did learn to ride a bike. When I had the "big fall", she felt it was a necessity to have a bike with brakes. In life, there are tears and laughter. Growing up is a challenge. As a child the love of life flows through us.

Laurel J. Freeman© 8/14/95

L♥vING

P
A
T
H
S

Chapter Introduction

Loving Paths are how I see our world. One ultimate question is: "Is life fair?" My answer is, "Yes". It is up to me to choose my attitudes on life, living, relationships, age, creativity and so on.

My motto is, "If I'm not having fun, why am I doing it?" For me life is full of wonderment and love.

I have had my share of disappointment, sorrow, sadness, anger and frustration. I have chosen to walk the loving paths. With each experience, I have used the information to move toward my highest good.

Many of these poems were written with someone special in mind. For me, all forms of life move on loving paths. By removing all the names you may enjoy the thought for itself. There is one exception, that being of my wonderful partner and mate, Howard. We walk our loving paths alone and together, simultaneously.

Enjoy living all your loving paths. ❤

Laurel J. Freeman© 7/26/99

As Howard Is To The World

Moving through the forest,
I greet all my family.
Mother deer, with eyes so gentle.
Opening my heart for
compassion and love of humankind.

Guided by my four, watching over me,
Allowing my free will.
For it is I alone,
Who moves along the path,
Who chooses the way to turn.

Gently embracing each I meet,
As brushed with a stroke of paint.
Opening their hearts to see
love and laughter,
Opening my heart to know.

My sorrows have been many,
For many of my forest family,
Have chosen distant plains.
Their teachings I have learned them well.
Their gift is love,
Which I have the opportunity to
Share with others.

Laurel J. Freeman© 9/22/96

By being the very best I can be.
By doing the very best with what I have.
By allowing the opportunity
To increase my awareness.

To let go of objects.
To know I have choices.
To embrace what I can not change.
My honesty rings loudly through the trees.

By example,
The honor bestowed upon me;
Is to show the forest to others.

I Love You!!! ❤

For Howard, the Love of My Life.

Laurel J. Freeman© 9/22/96

I Love Myself
The Way I Am

I love myself the way I am,
There's nothing I need to change.

I'll always be the perfect me,
There's nothing to rearrange.

I'm beautiful and capable of
Being the best me I can.
I love myself just the way I am.

I love you just the way you are,
There's nothing you need to do.

When I feel the love inside myself,
It's easy to love you.

Behind your fears, your rage and tears,
I see your shining star.
I love you just the way you are.

I love the world the way it is
'Cause I can clearly see,
That all the things I judge
Are done by people just like me.
So 'till the birth of peace on earth,
That only love can bring,
I'll help love grow by loving everything.

Laurel J. Freeman© 8/94

I love myself the way I am,
And still I want to grow.

The change outside can only come,
When deep inside I know,
I'm beautiful and capable of
Being the best me I can.

I love myself the way I am.
I love myself the way I am. ❤

Laurel J. Freeman© 8/94

The Eagle

Eagle, eagle hear my prayer, guide me to light,
The light that shines within me and others.

Eagle, eagle hear my prayer, guide me to strength,
The strength to open my heart and the ability
to share this with others.

Eagle, eagle hear my prayer, guide me to power,
The power to experience the unknown.

Eagle, eagle hear my prayer, guide me to love,
The love to encircle myself and others.
Eagle, eagle hear my prayer, guide me to see,
The sights beyond the seen.
Eagle, eagle hear my prayer, guide me to listen,
To sounds beyond the silence.

Eagle, eagle hear my prayer, guide me to experience,
To recognize feelings beyond the touch.

Your life mate by your side glides lovingly.
You soar with graceful wings spread wide,
Facing Mother Earth with open heart.
You follow the winds with ease,
Hearing sounds not made.
Seeing what cannot be seen.
Together, moving upward,
Majestically ever changing in the light.

Eagle, eagle hear my prayer.
May I follow your path. ❤

Laurel J. Freeman© 7/16/96

The Man

We just saw the movie "Chaplin".

Makes me want to read his autobiography.
He sees humor in everyday happenings,
which is really remarkable.

To want to change the world in some small way.

To leave such wonderful statements of life,
the human frailties and fragilities,
stretching the mind as far as one may,
wanting to leave the world in its
natural and safe form.

To think he felt he had failed,
missing the mark and not doing enough.

His was a life worth living,
reaching into the inner soul of another human.❤

How do we know when we have done enough to change humankind?

Laurel J. Freeman© 1/10/93

The Valley

We have come upon a valley,
Where the river flows deep and wide.
Where the land is plentiful,
Where the trees are full
and the hunting is abundant.
We have come upon a valley.
Where no human eyes have seen,
Where only the spirits have gathered,
Where many decisions were made.
This is the valley land
that when eyes
Hold fast
will take the body's breath.
Where green is ever green,
And blue is ever blue,
We have come upon a valley. ❤

---

*Written while in a Canadian Rocky Mountain park near Lake Louise.
The Indians spoke, they came to trade and gather here; where
the water meets and the game flourished. The ground was neutral
for trading, exchanging ideas, fishing and playing games.*

Laurel J. Freeman© 8/13/93

Me

I am healthy.

I may achieve what needs to be done.

I'm excited to see what life has to offer.

I know I may reach

out to

grasp anything

life holds for me. ❤

Laurel J. Freeman© 3/20/87

We Cried

We embraced in each others arms, two friends.
We cried.
For that moment in time, connecting.
We cried.
What does it all mean?
There is no rationale.
We cried.
Acknowledging existence. We cried.
For the loss of a mother. We cried.
For the loss of a daughter. We cried.
The comfort of knowing one another.
We cried.
Oh, to be left alone, the empty hollowness.
We cried.
Each wrapped in feelings no words can express.
We cried.
Encircled in memories.
We cried.
Tears of sadness mixed with flowing tears of joy.
We cried.
Opening our hearts to each other.
We cried.
Healing each other.
We cried.
Letting go, the ultimate challenge.
We cried.
And the love of life goes on.
We smiled. ❤

---

*A friend and I stood outside one evening, looking at the stars,
remembering loved ones. I went home and wrote this poem. The next morning in the
newspaper was the terrible news about an airplane crash in New York. We cried.*

Laurel J. Freeman© 7/17/96

Thanksgiving Thought

I look toward the sky
Filled with hues of grays and blues,
The morning star shines brightly
As night is put to sleep,

Day awakens to all the glory.
Joyful to be alive,
Today!
Here and now!

Oh, how I think of days gone by
Where we have come,
Where we are going.

Each day I give thanks
For each ray of sunshine,
The dew that glistens,
Smiling faces, opening hearts,
Holding hands, embracing arms,
The earth in which we walk, the trees,
The water bringing life to all,
The air we breathe.
Beams from the moon.

Life's so simple,
I give thanks.❤

Laurel J. Freeman© 11/26/96

From Above

Have you ever looked at clouds?
From the top?
Soft white cotton balls,
Only larger.

If you were to jump on one,
You just might bounce off to
Jump another.
Playing hop scotch all day
In the sky.

Yet,
As you fly through
They are
Rough, bumpy and grayish;
Unless the sun rays
Come shining in.
Casting shimmery, glistening
Pure white cotton mountain ranges,
Up close or seen in a distance.

Have you ever seen lightning?
From above looking down?
The most incredible light show
On Earth happens
When the brilliant yellow or white jagged crack appears.
The whole sky
Ripples in exquisite splendor.

Green, orange, red and blue
Sending a rainbow of colors throughout the sky.
By then the cotton balls have turned
Black and grayish
Adding to the panoramic view.

Have you ever seen the sky
From 33,000 feet up?
The blue is bluer and deeper,
The sky seems to go on forever.

Then there are layers,
Layers of clouds,
Long thin white streams
Drifting by.

As you look out,
White puffs of mountains
Speckle the horizon.

Further below,
Light gray valleys
With peaks and rounded like pebbles
From a hillside brook,
Softened through the years of time.

Sometimes, if the sun
Catches a cloud just right,
A rainbow will follow
Sifting through the mist.

Laurel J. Freeman© 8/5/90

If you have never witnessed
The sky from above
You are missing
One of the eight wonders of the world.

Interestingly enough,
Each time a plane takes off
And I view the scenery,
I realize a wondrous phenomenon.
The above looks so much
Like the below.
I'm glad I live in
This day and time
To have the opportunity
To experience
The heavens above.

Have you ever seen the earth?

From above looking down?

From close up above?

Or, far away above?

The trees are ever greener
Clusters of dense green with tops.
The lakes are clearly defined
Especially one that is familiar,
You may pick out every curve.

Laurel J. Freeman© 8/5/90

Homes look like a monopoly game.
Roads, paved streets and highways
Seem to know
Which direction to go.
You can always tell a well thought out town
Or subdivision.
The orderliness is impeccable,
Seen from above.

And cars, what a sight,
Like little cells running
Through our veins;
All knowing where to go,
Which way to turn.

But cows are the funniest!
They look like the little teeny tiny plastic toys
The dentist gives instead of lollipops.
Golf courses are organized green spaces.
And farmlands
Have wonderful hues of
Brown, red and green
Made into patchwork quilts.

Laurel J. Freeman© 8/5/90

Boats large and small
Always leave a trail.
And smaller planes or
Ones at lower altitudes,
Look like birds flying in
A straight line.

Exit ramps on highways look like
Giant figure eights.

As the wind blows,
The water
Shimmers with
Pure delight.

Swimming pools are
Dots of turquoise,
Nestled in the Earth.

OH! What a wondrous
Place this is.
Our Earth. ❤

I love to fly. Each time I go up, it is simply amazing to me how a plane flies and how awesome we and our planet are.

Laurel J. Freeman© 8/5/90

L♥vING

CHOICES

Chapter Introduction

L♥ving Choices is about knowing choice. By knowing there are choices, allows us to have more than one possibility. Each path has so many choices available.

Knowing I have the option to create is a wonderful gift. These choices enable me to have a deep appreication and love for life. Let us all walk our paths knowing and loving the gift of choice.

Our view of people, ideas, situations and the beautiful gifts of nature happen by choosing our attitude. By understanding there is choice, a person may choose how to move through life.

Love what you do and do what you love. That is choice. There are many ways to play with the meaning of loving choices. Our greatest gift to ourself is loving choices. The choice is ours. ❤

Changing Paths

When you first came into our lives,
We remember how bright and
Alive your eyes were.

Filled with youth and energy,
Sharp and willing to greet the world.

You brought with you a maturity,
Not matched by many.
Nothing would stand in your way.

You were ready for all life had to offer.

Through the years,
We watched you grow.
We laughed together,
Cried together,
Shared together.

You have typing quickness,
Ability to spell and to remember numbers,
To do many activities at once,
And to try new activities.
Now you have aged with years,
Your wisdom so much wiser,
Your vision so much broader.

All the qualities you first showed
Continue as you embrace excellence.

Laurel J. Freeman© 3/16/93

You have all the best
Life has to offer.

You will go far,
For you have discovered the secret,
"What you create, shall be yours."

Many years of success and happiness on
Every new adventure.♥

Laurel J. Freeman© 3/16/93

Behold

May the light of the sun's rays
shine into your heart,
As the waters flow through you.

May the moon beams glow on your presence,
As the waters flow over you.

May your essence be captured,
As the waters flow under you.

May your body's spirit soar,
As the waters in motion.

May your soul be found in your deeds to others,
As ever moving forms of change. ❤

Living Life

Life is like a dance.
We choose all the aspects of how
We flow to the rhythm.

We may choose to live in
Peace and harmony with ourselves.
This is one path to choose.

Your heart is pure and your soul is great,
Let them be your guiding forces.

Instead of doing what others say,
Know you have the option to listen to yourself.

For you will always guide yourself
To the path that takes you to your higher self.

Walk not in fear.
For when you are still,
You will act on thinking,
Not on reacting.

Trust yourself to do what is right for you.
You are a wonderful and loving person.

Laurel J. Freeman© 11/3/95

May you continue to channel all that you have.
In the best interest of yourself,
For then and only then,
Will self turn into selfless;
The true act of giving,
Which will shine through.

Be a leader to yourself.
Know in years to come,
People will flock to you for
Knowledge and strength.

First, you must find these
Qualities in yourself.
Your life will be as full as you choose,
When dancing to the rhythm.❤

Child Rearing 101

◆ From the beginning, teaching children
what they need to know is the most important
activity a parent may have. Become friends with
your children after they have learned what
they need to know (over age 16).

At any age:
◆ Allow them to make mistakes in a
safe and loving place.
◆ Give them all the love you can.
◆ We are all on loan to each other,
so be in the present.
◆ Decide what is important before saying "no".
◆ Teach choice,
as this is the beginning of wisdom.

◆ There is no such thing as the "terrible two's."
This is a new way of learning boundaries,
who has the last word and
how to communicate.

◆ Each year brings another
form of communication skills.

◆ Enjoy and have every day count.
These are the secrets of youth and success. ❤

For a friend's daughter, who just had a baby.

Laurel J. Freeman© 4/97

Yom Kippur Year 5757

Reflections of My Life

Each day is a new year,
24 hours
holds 1,440 minutes
holds 86,400 seconds.
What does this mean to me?

We humans decided that one day
is measured every time the
sun goes down and then comes up.

But, what if, the reality was, each second was a day?
Or, what if in reality, a day was one's total life span?

How, then, would we live our lives?
Would we add more meaning to each moment?
Would we care for one another with increased sensitivity?
Would we feel a need to help out with more enthusiasm?

What would we change?
Would we help ourselves to reach our highest goals?
Would we help others to do the same?

And is it true, he who dies with the most toys wins?
Or, is the one with love for self and others
who is remembered with embracing thoughts?

Is it the accumulation of things
that makes ones day meaningful?

Laurel J. Freeman© 9/22/96

Or, are the thoughts
of prophets and saints that one tries to emulate?

Is it quantity or quality?
Who is defining each?
What does "to be inscribed" really mean?

Collectively all our thoughts can change the world.
Individually all our thoughts can change the world.
Both move the masses.

I ask,
What is my charge to live each second?
My answer is, to be my very best,
With open heart, hand and mind.
Guided and guiding the way, to strive to be
my best each day of my life. ♥

In Judaism, Rosh Hashanah is the beginning of the new year. Then eight days later,
begins Yom Kippur which is the culmination of the new year. Unlike the traditional
Western new year celebration where people party the night away, Yom Kippur is
the last day in which a person has time to think and reflect on how to be
a better person before the next year.

Traditionally, this holiday is the most sacred and holy of all the holidays in the year.
My understanding is that people fast to focus away from the body and toward
the reflective process going on in order to be ready for the New Year. Since they have been
thinking for the last eight days on how to be a better person, it is their hope to be
inscribed or put into the "book of life".

The "book of life" means the person will be granted
another year to live, because that person has led a good life.

One Yom Kippur, a friend asked us to think ahead of time
what this day meant to us. These were my thoughts for a good life.

My definition of the word "best" is:
to do all I am capable of, with what I am able to comprehend at this moment.

Laurel J. Freeman© 9/22/96

The Shaman

He was a healer and spiritual leader among his people. A beautiful shaman came, with deep set eyes and high cheek bones, a soft, kind, powerful voice. His hair was long and flowing as it blew gently in the breeze.

The skin robe he wore was painted with inks of special berries, barks and leaves, made at a ceremony only for shamans. The markings and designs were elaborate and breathtaking.

On his open chest, he proudly wore a breast plate made of turquoise beads and white bone, interlaced with eagle feathers and falcon claws.

Upon his head was a mask of bear claws and mountain lion teeth, carefully arranged on a bison head. Both have been passed down from healer to healer for many generations.

In his right hand, he carried a shaker gourd on a decorated stick, with feathers of hawks and strips of leather dyed in many colors.

In his left hand he carried a pouch, filled with secret ritual objects. The pouch was usually worn around his neck. For this occasion, he held it firmly yet gently in his palm to bring more power to his words.

This is what the Shaman shared:

A wise one once said,
"You will take a journey.

As you travel these paths,
you will come to forks.
Which ever paths you choose,
Are the right ones.

You will climb over mountains and dales.
You will go through deep valleys.
You will pass through forests and glens.
You will go through streams and rivers.

There will be rains that flood and snows too deep,
Many moons will pass.
As days grow short and long.
Your hair will lengthen and change in color.

As you travel
You will gain the strength of the bear,
The wisdom of the lion,
The knowledge of an elephant,
The health of a snake.

You will journey toward the Sun,
Whose rays will shine upon you."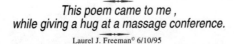

This poem came to me ,
while giving a hug at a massage conference.
Laurel J. Freeman© 6/10/95

Life Force

I cling to the rocks below with my roots
Holding on as many pass me by
My roots intertwining into the soil.
I may be the last of my kind.
I must survive.
I must.

There are many trees in the forest,
Where the green moss and algae grows.
I may be the last of my kind.
I must survive.
I must.

Boldly I weather the snow and the frost,
The heat and the rain and the drought.
I may be the last of my kind.
I must survive.
I must.

Oh, the stories I have heard of this and that,
Some come by to stand and chat.
I may be the last of my kind.
I must survive.
I must.

Some stand by for comfort and shade
Some stop for repose or to snack or to drink
Some come just to hear or to think.
I may be the last of my kind.
I must survive.
I must.

And here I stand so tall and round,
All alone, yet making a group.

A group of one.

And all I know is no matter what,
I may be the last of my kind.
I must survive.
I must. ❤

*Coming back from a hike in Glacier National Forest,
we came upon a tree growing on its side.
It was amazing how it could survive with the root system
open to the elements and the rocks pushing it up.*

Laurel J. Freeman© 8/4/96.

A Universal Truth

One in heart and in mind
respect oneself.

We never really know
what profound effect
we have on others.

It is one's power and strength
which makes
each of us
special and unique.

To exist
it is important to touch
another in some way.

Fortunately,
we have many avenues
from which to choose
these paths. ❤

*My definition of "A Universal Truth" is a thought or statement which in all
realities will always be true. When tested it always comes out positive.*

Laurel J. Freeman© 6/8/97

and....

Lift up thine eyes

and

see

unto

thy

self. ❤

....More

Reaching

out

to find
the

gold

in

everyone. ❤

---

*The following are thoughts that have come
to mind through the years.*

Laurel J. Freeman© 3/7/89, 5/5/88

....and

My definition of massage:

The Lacquer

on the

Perfect

Sculpture.

A Universal Truth:

When one

lets go

of

control

completely,

more control

is

achieved. ❤

Laurel J. Freeman© 5/5/88, 11/10/90, 6/8/97

55

Discussion

What does our brain
actually do with all the
information it receives?

Why would we want some of
those so-called facts anyway?

I sometimes ponder on
such trivialities,
knowing the answer
will never be resolved.
Like a game I may play,
to rest
from all the other happenings
in the world. ❤

Universal Truth on Interpersonal Communication

Intelligence
is the ability
to
access
great techniques and skills,
to explore
all ideas
and
then
apply the concepts internally. ❤

56

Laurel J. Freeman© 4/27/88, 12/15/84

Great

If everyone would

be selfish

by giving the gift of giving

to someone else,

What a great world

this would be. ♥

Where Did It Go?

I know this may sound silly.
I bought
a roll of
invisible tape.
And now
I can not find it. ♥

Laurel J. Freeman© 10/8/93, 3/18/86

My Wish

In some

small

way,

I would like to think

i

have made

a

difference. ❤

Laurel J. Freeman© 9/8/93

L♥VING

RAINBOWS

Chapter Introduction

L♥ving Rainbows come from seeing the world as a wonderment of color and sensations. All the choices life has to offer and the joyful gifts we give to each other are our rainbows. The more gifts we give, the more rainbows we receive. Someone's smile, the warming of my heart, the sand beneath my feet and the soft grass tickling my toes are some of those rainbows.

L♥ving Rainbows are the multi dimensional spectrum of life that stimulate and excite me. This allows me the feeling of being alive. I like to think I am always ready to go and see what is out there.

Looking at rainbows gives each of us our own experience. Being present to see the rainbows allows us to experience life to its fullest. By knowing there is choice, we are given the opportunity to see many sides of the rainbow. ♥

Laurel J. Freeman© 8/27/99.

Gift Wrapped
"Rainbow Bubbles"

Every morning around four a.m. or so,
I send out good thoughts to people,
Some I don't even know.
I wrap them up in rainbow bubbles,
then send them out all over the world.

For those who seem to have troubles.
To those who are starving and have no home.
To those who are sick and all alone.
To those who are dying to find the strength.
To those who are left to carry on.
To close friends who need a helping hand.

Love and kindness are the themes,
For each person will get what they need.
Sending rainbow bubbles gives such purpose.
In some small way,
Reaching and making a difference.

I know it works, for some will call,
Not knowing I've sent bubbles at all.
I pick up the phone to hear them say,
"Just a quick hello" or
"I was thinking of you today".

Laurel J. Freeman© 1/10/93

Sometimes, I call ahead to let friends know,
If something splashes or they feel a glow,
I am sending them rainbow bubbles,
Full of love and good thoughts,
To follow them wherever they go.

Each of us has the ability
to make these bubbles,
And how they get sent is unique to us all.
Wrapped from our hearts,
We may send them out in our own special way.
Anyone may send a bubble or two,
The more we send, the easier it gets.
It is so much fun, anytime will do.
If everyone just sent one or two,
They would make our day special and
someone else's, too.
Gift wrapped "rainbow bubbles"
are the thing to do.❤

In 1988, I started sending rainbow bubbles.
Every morning I wake up around 4 a.m.,
instead of forcing myself back to sleep, I just send rainbow bubbles,
Sometimes I send over 500 bubbles,
First, I send one to myself, then Howard my husband and then to
family, friends, countries or wherever healing is needed;
knowing the rainbow bubbles will "pop" on someone and they will feel the love.

 62

Laurel J. Freeman© 1/10/93

Morning Prayer

I lie with arms to my side,
palms gently turned upward.
I breathe.
Oh, Father Sky,
Shower me with all your riches.
I am open to receive
your wisdom, justice, love,
wonder, and outer strength.
I breathe.
Oh, Mother Earth,
Wrap me in your arms.
So I may receive
your wisdom, justice, love,
patience and inner strength.
I breathe.
And in return,
I will bring to others
what you have shared with me.
Wisdom, justice, love, wonders,
patience, outer and inner strengths.
This is my oath. ❤

I wrote this at 4 a.m., while at a massage convention.
Later we learned that one of Howard's cousins had died that morning.

Laurel J. Freeman© 7/18/93

Mirrors

We are the mirrors

that reflect each others light,

crystallizing the

beauty

of the

invisible,

bringing us

to

sight. ❤

The Wish

May the people
who live on this earth
learn to walk
together in
harmony,
peace,
love,
laughter
and
friendship. ❤

We went to a Japanese Rite of Spring Party at a friend's home.
There was a tree to hang wishes on. This was and still is my wish.

Laurel J. Freeman© 4/27/88, 3/29/96

Open Hands

The forests are forever growing,
I open my hands to feel.

The mountains are forever changing,
I open my hands to hear.

The streams, rivers and oceans
are forever flowing,
I open my hands to see.

The air is forever moving,
I open my hands to sense.

To feel what is not there,
To hear what is not said,
To see what cannot be seen,
To sense all the love there is.

I open my hands,
To the oneness of all. ❤

Coming back from a hike in Glacier National Forest.

Laurel J. Freeman© 8/4/96

Thanksgiving

As the past
          becomes the present
          becomes the future
          becomes the past
                    so the spiral moves
          and
                    our awareness alters.

Let us gather together,
          to acknowledge we are all one.

          As we unite in harmony,
Let us bring strength,
          courage and love to others.
Let us heal our Mother Earth.
Let us experience our own abilities.
Let us create a world
In which we work and play together.
          Let us stop the war.
          Let us send helping thoughts to those in need.
To let them know we are
          here together
          and we care.
The past, present and future are all one. ❤

Laurel J. Freeman© 11/24/94

TURNING CORNERS

Chapter Introduction

Turning Corners is about everyday events such as birthdays and celebrations of all kinds. Living life is creating change. While we think we are on a direct path, we are actually turning corners along the way.

Corners are the experiences that make life interesting and inspiring. To be at a corner is a wonderful space and place to be. Turning keeps us moving, like the flowing tide, the rising Moon, the setting Sun. Turning corners are the dances of life.

All of these poems were written with someone special in mind. To me, each person was turning corners in the dance of life. So you may experience this dance, I removed all the names with the exception of our beautiful daughter, Carolyne, as a tribute to her and the meaning she has brought into my life dance. ❤

Carolyne

On your birthday I sat and thought,
of all the years gone by,
We have come to know each other.

On the first day, I held you so small and fine,
We looked into each others eyes.
I, wondering what you were thinking.
How incredible life is.

Then as you grew, which did not take long,
You formed ideas and ways of doing things,
Different than my own.
How does that happen, I wondered?
And it was good.

We have traveled roads not covered by others,
Though others may come to the same path.
We weave our paths in and out of time
Some passing once or maybe twice.
We each seem to go on our own special journey,
Unique, together yet alone.

And now a quarter of a century has flown,
Right before me, in one short breath.
In years of growing, growth and grown,
You have arrived on the doorsteps of life.

Laurel J. Freeman© 8/23/93.

Full of knowledge, warmth,
Lovingness and beauty,
Full of empathy, intelligence and
Strengths in many ways,
Too many to list.

And, I knowing,
The more I know,
The less I know.
My, how the wonders of
The world works.

We have entwined
Each other forever,
My dear Daughter,
Who has taught me so much.

I honor and embrace life.
I honor and embrace you.

I encourage you to enjoy all the embracing
Life has to offer,
At the beginning and through the years.
Your new year is the
Beginning of an everyday embrace. ❤

Forever Always Love,
Your Mom

For our wonderful Daughter on her 25th Birthday.

Laurel J. Freeman©8/23/93

Birthday Year

May all your days,
rise in silver and gold;
As clear as the Sun,
as bright as the Moon.
May you see all your
dreams come true.
May the mountains you cross,
give you strength.
May the valleys you come to,
give you peace.
May we enjoy each others
company in many years to come.

Have a Wonderful Birthday year. ❤

I believe Birthdays are to be celebrated all year, and each day is another birthday.

Laurel J. Freeman© 3/20/94

Live Life and Take Heart

There was a young man, Israel his homeland.
We all know his name, a doctor he became.

To help people get well, to make their lives swell
To give them hope, to help them cope.

He met a beautiful woman nurse,
We all know her name.
He courted and pursued, until she was wooed.

So happily married, with a life so varied.
The world they traveled,
Making Gainesville their home.

With a heart that over worked and
Had its quirks.
The road he traveled,
Would make the average unraveled.
Strong and steadfast, he went forth.
To the battlefield of life itself.
He fought like Sir Gallahad and
Conquered the heart he once had.

Now with vim and vitality,
He is ready to set forth on new found sea.

With new perspective and friends to share;
Long life to you;
With many birthdays to spare. ❤

Laurel J. Freeman© 1/16/93

The Process

Life is a process.
Moving, bending, extending, searching.
When one finds the center,
It is like a sonar signal,
Once in place,
The sound of oneness radiates outward.

It is only when we look in,
That we can have the opportunity
To see out with clarity.

The process of life is:
To know the opportunities,
To move in harmony,
To bend as the flow of the tide,
To extend knowing, growth will resonate,
To search for choices,
To find what is within our hearts,
To know and believe in the path chosen.

Each year,
Your life process aligns you
Closer to the process of life.
You are and can be.❤

Laurel J. Freeman©9/22/96

Birthday Knowledge

Birth is the start.
We live
and
We learn to love.
We come to know
Age
Is a state of mind.

Wisdom comes from knowing.
Growing requires
the knowledge of wisdom
and
the knowledge of love.

This
Is the beginning.

Happy 50th with many more to come.❤

Laurel J. Freeman© 4/12/97.

Birthday Friends

Every now and then,
We meet a person who becomes a friend.

These friends do not pass by everyday.
Friends are committed to each other.

Though they may only see each other
Every now and then,
And be parted by distance;
Friends are still connected.

You are such a person.

Thank you for your friendship.
May this birthday be the best first day!

And may each day
Continue to be great for
The rest of your life.

Your Friend, Love ❤

Beginning

Fifty is the beginning
of the age
of enlightenment
and so
begins your journey.

This is the time
to gather
all your resources and
utilize this knowledge
to bring into
your life, wisdom.

May your journey
be with
ease and grace
love and laughter
knowing and known forever. ❤

Laurel J. Freeman© 6/7/97.

You Are Love

You are love.
Dancing through life
Opening, swaying,
Moving to the beat of your heart.

You are love.
Family intertwines your threads of gold.

You are love.
Two of you glowing
sparkling as the dawn awakens.

You are love.
Values like the granite rocks
Firm and strong and present.

You are love
As the stars shine each night
showering you with love.

You are lovingly, loved;
As you love. ❤

Laurel J. Freeman© 6/22/97.

Birthday Card

Happy Birthday!
You are one of the most
giving and loving persons
we know.

Thank you for sharing
yourself with us.

And thank you for giving us
the opportunity to
celebrate your special day.

We look forward
to many more to come.❤

Laurel J. Freeman© 9/8/96.

Some Stay The Same

As the years come and go,
He's still in the know.

We have watched him swim,
To finish with a great win!

Two girls who are his pride and joy,
And a camera his special little toy.

Oh, the pictures he did take and
Many a journey his lovely wife and he did make.

They traveled near and far,
And not just in that old green car.

When ordering a drink, you see,
He only orders a thirst quenching Pepsi.
The pond had a special meaning,
as the fish disappeared with the bird agleaming.

With gardening and landscaping under your belt,
How about learning to dance 'till you melt?
A truer friend no one can find,
For he would give you his last and only dime.

Three cheers to you,
and another 50 plus,
A celebration with you is a must!
Happy 50th birthday and Many More! ❤

Growing

You are a wonderful person.
We have watched you grow since the beginning.

Through the years you have developed
many great qualities:
your compassion for others,
your energy for life,
your desire to learn and to expand
your mind and your love.
May you continue to increase all these things.

Thank you for sharing
yourself with us. ❤

Laurel J. Freeman© 12/94

Living

We admire you so
Traveling far and traveling wide,
Hill and dale and countryside.

Not a moment to lose,
You didn't miss a trick,
From terrific bridge to the great golf stick.

Friends are many and family tight,
You live your life
With great delight. ❤

Aunt Fannye's birthday was on March 7, 1995. She was very ill and wanted to have a party. We all went to the party and had a great visit with her. This poem was read to her at the party. She died on June 16, 1995.

Laurel J. Freeman© 3/7/95

The River

You are Great!!
We loved all
the warmth, kindness and genuine love
your beautiful family shares with others
and you are no exception.
You are the rule!!

What a wonderful gift you have to share.
Thank you for being you!
Your party was fantastic.
Love was everywhere,
laughter and sharing.
What a super time!!!

May you continue on the path
you have set for yourself,
knowing as the river flows
there will be bends, twists and turns,
ever moving as life carries you forth.
Like the river Jordan,
we know you will handle whatever
comes your way! ❤

Laurel J. Freeman© 12/17/94

Doc

Working hard and having fun,
It is amazing all you have done.

Traveling far and wide,
Always ready for a wondrous ride.

A wife, and mother of two;
Always in "the pink" and never blue.

A pilot you are ready to fly,
Over the hill and into the sky.

With your expert karate chop,
It is said, "You can make a grown man drop!!"

In work you share,
Of teaching love through nursing care.

A doctorate does not come in a day;
It is perseverance and determination
all the way.

We are so proud of all you do;
Doctor
Three cheers to You!!! ❤

Special

To someone very special,
Who we've known a long, long time.
The miles we've swum together,
And the parties, oh, so fine.

You held on
And stuck it out,
Through thick and thin.
We knew you could do it,
We knew you could win!

On those lonely days,
When you could have been dreary,
Through all the laughter and the tears,
You always kept yourself cheery.

This is a special birthday,
And we're so proud of YOU.
Wishing you the best.
We toast more years of friendship,
Health and happiness, too.♥

Laurel J. Freeman© 9/16/88

Bear

Bear,
Your inner soul.

Bear
Knows no fear.

Bear
Knows only power and strength.

Bear
Brings healing to the land.

Bear
Is well and safe.

Bear
Allows peace and harmony.

Walk with the
Bear. ❤

Laurel J. Freeman© 7/5/94

Fifty Birthdays

As you come of age,
The number 50 comes to mind.
Five is the beginning of transition,
Zero the beginning of time.
Fifty moves you in a new direction,
Viewing each idea with eyes unfolding.
New with the familiar,
New with each emotion,
New with thought.

Fifty is a letting go,
Fifty is seeing the truth in all,
With no attachments.
May you open
Your heart and
Walk with power and dignity.
And on your journey,
Fifty will forever
Embrace
You in
Love. ❤

Laurel J. Freeman© 7/12/95

Moving

The drum beats to the
heart of the sound.

The oneness of the universe
With majestic vastness.

The power of allowing choices,
Rhythmically
Changing
The spirit within.

May you have
a lovely birthday
with many
happy days to continue
your celebration. ❤

Laurel J. Freeman© 7/5/96

Opening

Every now and then
a special person walks the earth.

Unfolding
her arms,
spreading love,
joy and warmth.
To all she meets,
as a rose opens for all to share.

You are that special person.
Howard and I are honored to know
you and call you a friend.
Thanks.

May you have a very
Happy Birthday
and
May we share
many more to come. ❤

Laurel J. Freeman© Year Unknown

Forty

He rocks, he rolls, He even strolls.
Go, _____, Go!

A strut, a stride, A slide, a glide.
Go, _____, Go!

He yells, he sells, He puts on bells.
Go, _____, Go!

He walks, He talks, He knows his hawks.
Go, _____, Go!

Friends, friends, What friends he has.
Go, _____, Go!

A family man, Yes siree.
Go, _____, Go!

Hobbies, cars and bugs, He loves to give hugs.
Go, _____, Go!

See him here, See him there.
Go, _____, Go!

From six to forty, Oh, Lordy, Lordy.
Go, _____, Go!

Many more to come, We love all the fun.
Go, _____, Go!

Happy 40th!!! ❤

On the Go

She dances through the night,
Her basketball is out-a-sight.

Her ping-pong is a fling,
Oh boy, can she sing.

She plays volleyball,
both in water and on land,
which is simply just grand.

Her overhead smash in racquetball is a killer,
Just watch the game for a thriller.

A tax attorney, "extraordinaire"
Add in bridge and it's just not fair.

A volunteer who has the time,
Gee, she's mighty fine.

To give a hug and a friendly cheer,
Oh! Yes, forty, such a great year!!

We Love You! ♥

Laurel J. Freeman© 4/27/92

Congratulations

Congratulations!
May you set
your sails into
open waters
and
experience all that
life has to offer,
The laughter,
The sorow,
The love,
The joy.

All are choices on
how to view an experience.

Choices are wonderful.

Live with no regrets
and
love your choices.

Much love in the years to come! ❤

Laurel J. Freeman© 5/3/97

Can You Believe?

When he plays poker,
He goes for broke.
When he plays basketball,
He goes for the throat.

When he plays golf,
It is no joke.
Gone fishin', you say,
He's on his way.

It seems no quirk,
There is no time for work.
What a bundle of fun,
All rolled up into one.
Off he goes to New York and PA,
Sometimes London, Europe and LA.

Jaguar, Wow! What a car!
Too bad it doesn't go very far.
He has two great kids, lucky for him,
Otherwise, things could have been grim.

House projects through the years,
Have drawn blood, sweat and tears.
She happens to be the best part of his life,
Only because she is his wife.

Me oh my, to be so bold,
Can you believe, he's half-a-century old?
Love, your friends, for the next half century.❤

Laurel J. Freeman© 4/28//90

The 50 Game

Fifty is the name,
And life is the game.

A very special caring Doctor for hearts,
Please don't eat any beans,
for they cause you the ___.

His nose has had practice,
with kleenex and air,
A nose that big is just not fair.

With stocks and bonds,
no one can comparish,
He is fantastic with bullish, or is it bearish?

Watch for the ski slopes of Aspen,
That down hill run was great,
just ask 'im.

The bike can be deadly,
as we all can remember,
Any bike trips planned for the month of December?

On bikes to France and Belgium all the way
Making love with his wife in the rolling hay.
Montana, mountains, canyon and dale,
He rides through the west,
like a bat out of ___.

Laurel J. Freeman© 11/30/92

Spiritually each year,
he is growing and growing,
As the years pass, he seems to be glowing!

A wise man once said,
"It is important to be fed."

With that in mind,
keep that chocolate coming,
So you know who can keep right on humming.

With beautiful bride by his side,
he cannot go wrong,
The next fifty years will be a happy song!

Years come and go,
and birthdays, too.
It is wonderful to find a great friend like
YOU!

Happy Birthday
And many more to come! ❤

Laurel J. Freeman©11/30/92

The Graduate

Now you are a Graduate,
This is your time.

Oh! How great is the
Class of '89'

Your friends of old will come and go;
With new friends waiting for you to know.

In the years to come,
You may miss your high school days,
In only small ways.
But don't let anything bring you down.

Think of the future that lies ahead,
Go out there and
Knock 'em dead! ❤

Love

In 1989, six of our friend's children graduated from high school. Instead of getting them a card, I made up this poem to give with their gift.

Laurel J. Freeman© 6/10/89

Jumping Hoops

You have spent your life growing and learning,
But college gave you such a yearning.

So off to school, you did go,
Not to tarry to and fro.

For all those all-nighters,
You burned the candles even brighter.

For all those days you thought to quit,
You were not swayed and kept your wit.

For all the days the books you read,
Your cat sometimes did not get fed.

For each day is only a moment in time,
You are here today and feeling fine.

For all the hours you worked away,
Now, is the time for some fun and play.

For all the years you waited 'til...
Today is the day for the greatest thrill.

You did it, you did it all,
Graduated, Now have a ball! ♥

Laurel J. Freeman© 5/15/93

Together

Some are together forever
Through all types of weather.
You shall never meet another pair
With whom you can compare.

For over the world they did travel
Near and far on all kinds of gravel.
Playing their way through the game of life
Making it through any kind of strife.

Not only playing tennis,
instruments and any kind of game
They keep on winning more fortune and fame.

She's always at the gym
Looking mighty healthy and trim.
And he keeps right on biking
For exercise and his own liking.
There is no slowing them down
Inspirations to all in the town.

Happy Birthday to You Both,
We are as happy as can be
Three Cheers to You,
In Nineteen ninety-three! ❤

Continuing

With all the things you can do,
Me oh my! There is no time to be blue.

As 50 comes round, you will abound.
With a tennis racquet, you're out of any bracket.
The charm of your flute, can be heard by a mute.

And sailing, oh sailing!
What a breeze,
Great with any boat
And gee, what a tease!

On land, by sea or in the air, you do it all with such a flair.
Without the help of your fair mother,
Surely, you would have been just another.

So now that your older and wiser for sure,
You know life has just started to pull the lure.
With a beautiful wife by your side, you cannot go wrong,
The next 50 years will be a happy song!

For you will sing, play, sail and glide
Having as much fun as the ocean tide.

Celebrate today,
We're sending hugs and kisses
And a BIG HURRAY!
Happy Birthday
And many more to come! ❤

Laurel J. Freeman© 9/12/93

Strength and Grace

As we all grow old and gray;
Some people stay the same young way.

Not a year has passed, on your face;
You are full of strength and grace.

Me, oh my, the years have flown by;
Don't even think to ask us why.

We are lucky to have friends so great;
It is nice to know we can even be late.

And so another year has come,
You know how to do it right by having fun!!❤

Laurel J. Freeman© 9/30/90

Special One

When a person as special as you,
Touches our lives, there are no words

That can share:
The thoughts, the smiles,
The laughs, the hopes,
The teachings, the dreams,
The love, the care,

You have shown to many others.

You have energy which abounds,
While others may stop to rest.

You have found the time for living,
As others let life pass them by.

You have done what one must do,
When others could not.

Our life is only a speck in time,
And you have accomplished so much.

With wings spread wide,
You soar through the skies.
Be not afraid as you travel along,
For you are not alone.

Know that we are all one with the universe.
Know what others will never know,
You are a special one. ❤

Laurel J. Freeman© 8/24/92

LOOKING for SILVER ...or GOLD

Chapter Introduction

Looking for Silver or Gold is the goal of living life with another. Anniversaries and other events are a common happening, yet our society only celebrates the day. I believe in celebrating each moment.

It is amazing when two people are in a relationship and choose to communicate. This is a grand accomplishment!

I have a long theory about marriage; this is the short version. I believe the institution of marriage is old and until recently has not been tested to its capacity. One hundred years ago, people did not live as long. For the most part, men were running off to war and/or to conquer and see unknown lands. Many men did not return, many found another life and many realized, in some situations, it would take the rest of their life to return home.

The whole concept of staying with one person for many years is really a foreign concept to our DNA structure. I have been told that it takes a period of time equal to four generations to create long term change.

To communicate with another person is an honor. It is very exciting when two people have the opportunity to experience love and communicate this love experience. I honor and applaud those who are helping to create change.♥

Laurel J. Freeman© 8/27/99

I Do

With hearts and flowers,
you counted the hours
St. Valentine's Day sent
you on your married way.

Your journey has taken you
to foreign lands and many seas;

To travel along the conscious road,
to open doors.

To workshop you abound, gathering the tools;
To see the gardens of the subconsciousness.

You will reach into one another; for the growth,
Respect, and understanding.
Learning to trust and trust in the learning;

To give strength,
to show care with love.
These are the highest gifts of heavens above.

It is the everyday life,
the here and now.

These are the vows said twenty-three years ago,
"I DO!" ❤

Together

Happy Anniversary
and many more to come!!
You are a great couple.

We love the special times
we have shared together
and
look forward to adding
many more memories.

May your years together
be filled with
love,
laughter,
sharing,
caring and
much happiness!!!

We love you.❤

Laurel J. Freeman© 3/17/96

Special

May all your days be filled with
love, laughter, and happiness.

We love having such
a special friendship with
two wonderful people
like you.

May our friendship continue
to grow as
your love for each other
grows stronger.

Many more anniversaries
to come.
Many more
laughs and
many more
great years
together.

We love you.❤

Laurel J. Freeman© 3/17/97

The Wedding

May all your
dreams and hopes come true
and become your reality.

May your home
be filled with
laughter,
love
and
happiness.

May you always come to agreement
with love and respect
by knowing yourself and each other
you will bring your own experiences
into this relationship.

We wish you all the best. ❤

Laurel J. Freeman© 10/21/95

Twenty-Five

Sweethearts as teenagers,
True love at first sight.

Having fun together,
All day and all night.

Two beautiful kids
Provide your shining light,
Making your family just right.

Working and playing for 25 years.

Wishing you well,
And many great cheers.

We look forward
To celebrating
Many more years. ❤

Laurel J. Freeman© 6/1/96

Engagement

May you sail
through life
together
filled with
health and happiness.

May you ride
the waves
and
round the shores
with a spirit
to meet
the challenges
in love and laughter.

We wish you
all the best
with everything!! ❤

Laurel J. Freeman© 1/29/95

New Day

May your life together
be as glowing as
the kaleidoscope.

May your love
be never ending
in your joy
for each other.

We love you
and are with you
in spirit on
your wedding day. ❤

Laurel J. Freeman© Date Unknown

Newly Weds

You are the wonderful bride,
Who will always have sweet hubby
By your side.

He is the groom,
Who makes thorough use
Of his own special room.

Both of you have come a long way,
To have and to hold
Each other everyday.

Two special people you are.
We know your happiness
Will go far.

Live in harmony and health
And may the future bring you both
Spiritual and financial wealth. ❤

Laurel J. Freeman© 11/26/88

Celebrate

Every day we may celebrate life
And your 25th Anniversary
Is wonderful indeed.
Those you have gathered
makes this an extra treat.
We look forward to
the many years to come
Thank you for sharing this special time,
Your Happy Anniversary,

with many more to celebrate! ❤

Years of Love

On our wedding a few years thence,
Full of excitement and wonderment,
We began a new life to make some sense.

Where have all these years flown?
Just think, it has only been a few.
Oh my, how we have grown.

The laughter, the tears, the struggles and happiness,
Throughout these short fifty years.

Our precious children so wonderful
Thank you for the opportunity to watch them
Grow, live, and become successful.

Wanting to help take any pain away,
And yet, knowing they needed to grow
In their own special way.

Then the grandchildren so special to us.
We saw the caring and love,
So proud of our children and all the fuss.
Over Eighteen Thousand Two
Hundred and Fifty days
Filled with new adventure and companionship,
Two friends still in love.

Playing tennis, volunteering and growing,
And keeping the love in our hearts still
Glowing! ❤

Laurel J. Freeman© 11/25/88

Wedding Poem
Version 1

We were happy to hear,
When the wedding news came here,
That you were joining together.

We hope that you, too,
Will be as happy as we two.

And your years together,
Will last forever!

Many years of
Love, Laughter, Health and Happiness. ❤

See Version 2 in the next chapter.

bRIDGIng

PATHWAYS

Chapter Introduction

Bridging Pathways is my way of honoring others who have expressed themselves on paper. Words are a powerful tool.

We all have an opportunity to write what we are thinking or feeling. Many of us would choose to share, if there was an avenue in which to do so.

These poems and thoughts are from family and friends. As I walk my path, presenting avenues for expression by others is important. ❤

Laurel J. Freeman© 8/27/99

Thanksgiving Day

Our Heavenly Father,
We thank you for giving us this wonderful
opportunity for being together
with our friends and family
on this day of Thanksgiving.

We ask for your continual guidance
to learn the true meaning of life,
in appreciation of our loved ones and our friends,
in respect each others desires,
To grow as good spiritual human beings,
helping others less fortunate.
To achieve a more meaningful life.

We thank you for letting us spend
many happy times with our loved ones
who left this earth for greater challenges.

We thank you for sharing
their wonderful spirits with us.

May we continue to grow and
become better human beings.

We simply say thank you
for giving us so much. Amen. ❤

This prayer was written by Howard for one of our Thanksgiving Gatherings.

Howard G. Freeman© Date Unknown

 117

To My Loveable Dad

Dear Dad,
I wrote this little poem
Because I wanted you to know,
What you do for me.
Besides, your my lovable Dad!
When I'm down, there you are.
Trying to cheer me up with your jokes.
Sometimes you succeed, sometimes you don't.
But, I don't care as long as I know you are there.
When I need you,
I have no doubt;
That you will be there.
Because your my lovable Dad!
Boy, I'm lucky to have a lovable Dad!
Too bad everyone doesn't.
I would share you,
But, you're too much my treasure,
To ever give you away.
Besides, your my lovable Dad!
When I'm bored,
You give me a lot of things to do,
Even if I don't like them.
I'll do them for you,
Because you are my lovable Dad!
When I go to sleep
But I can't sleep,
You come in and make up one of your stories.
Next thing I know-
We're both asleep.

Bonnie R. Freeman© 5/30/82

'Till you start snoring.
But don't worry Dad,
I don't mind getting woken up.
By my lovable Dad!
Well, now you know.
You do a lot for me, that's
Why I really wrote this,
was because I wanted you to know,
I love my lovable Dad!! ❤

Love,
Bonnie

---

*Our daughter, Bonnie, had leukemia and was having a bone marrow
transplant in 1982 during Father's Day. Since she could not go out to buy a gift,
I suggested she write him something. I slept on a cot in her hospital room.
One morning around 3AM, she woke up to go to the bathroom. She asked to take
paper and pencil. At 6AM, the nurse came in to take Bonnie's vital signs and did not
see her. Upon waking me, we found Bonnie in the bathroom writing this poem.
She put it on a big piece of construction paper which we have framed in Howard's study.
Bonnie died on July 10, 1983.*

Bonnie R. Freeman© 5/30/82

Thanksgiving Shower

Thanksgiving Day is our favorite of the year,
It gathers family and friends from far and near.

An old American tradition,
In 1619 was the first rendition.

In 1789, Washington issued a declaration,
By 1863, Lincoln made it a federal celebration.

At harvest time, when food is ripe,
The squashes, apples, potatoes and like,
With love and care are fixed just right.

Give thanks for memories and those we hold dear,
Make a great day for all to cheer.

What more can we say?
Than, wish you a healthy and happy,
Thanksgiving Day! ❤

*Our friend's daughter was having a shower. Each person invited was given a holiday and
the gift was to represent that time. The theme choosen for us was Thanksgiving.
We purchased items needed for Thanksgiving such as
a roaster, potato masher, strainer, etc. Carolyne and I wrapped all the
presents in the form of a turkey in the roasting pot.
We laughed all the way to the shower.
How did they know this was our favorite holiday?
I only know, the universe works in wondrous ways.*

Laurel and Carolyne Freeman © 3/5/94

Wedding Poem
Version 2

This is your special day!
Soon you will be on your married way.
As the bell chimes the hour,
We see you glistening as lovely as
a spring shower.
Your vows of marriage have been taken,
As life anew has awakened.
Your life's story will unfold the rest.
We wish you all of the very best!

Many years of
Love, Laughter, Health and Happiness. ❤

Cosmic Intimations

Do you think among the Pleiades
We'll find more wisdom than had Maimonides?

Or hear sweeter music to sustain us
On sundrenched Dipper, Mars or Venus?

Why must we travel to the farthest star?

Let's find our bearings near not far.

Come home,
my love,
by love's course true,
With sparkling eye and honeyed mouth,
You'll find home here for
I love you. ❤

Written by our Mom, Breezy Freeman, in memory of her wonderful, fun and loving sister, Bernice, who died in January of 1995. Pleiades is a cluster of stars in the constellation of Taurus. Maimonides was a Spanish-Jewish scholar and philosopher, who lived from 1135-1204, during the time of the Spanish Inquisition.

Breezy Freeman© 1/16/95

Plans

In moon mist memory
We planned our days
To live just near enough
To say "Hello"
And share a cup of tea.

Just close enough
Yet still to hoard
Our precious privacy.

How could I dream
That when you died
You would be bold enough
To storm the bastion of my fragile heart?

You willed your life to live in me
Gossamered, in sublime intimacy.

Hold fast!
I surrender to you forever,
My dear forever
VALENTINE. ❤

---

*Gossamer is a fine filmy cobweb seen on grass and bushes
or floating in the air in calm weather.*

Breezy Freeman© 2/14/93

Doris
Our "We Love You" Poem

Doris is the name
Keeping busy is the game.

Never a moment to lose,
Coming and going as you choose.

Writing, traveling and music, too,
Oh, there is so much to do.

Volunteering is a special sport,
Doing for all with full support.

Seventy-Two, yip-py-i-yeh,
It sure doesn't come along everyday.

So we have joined here to say,
Have a very Happy Birthday! ❤

We Love You,
THE GANG

Doris is a wonderful addition to our family. For the past several years we celebrate her birthday with an unsurprise, surprise party. The years have flown by and Doris is as active as ever, doing all the activities she can fit in during each day.

Howard, Laurel and Carolyne Freeman© 11/11/92

We Dance

You and I
Us
Together
Yet separate
As one
We dance

The dance of life
Beyond life
In life
Swirling, bending
With motion
Without motion
Inside
Outside
Connected
Still
Silent

You are me
I am you
Yet we are not each other
Together
We dance! ❤

Amber has been a friend for many years. We have a great time being massage therapists and discuss topics such as the wonders of living and how we all fit into the scheme of life.

Amber Waters© 11/6/97

The Client

The elements have aligned
The perfect day
The perfect hour
She arrives this time
Without an agenda
Or expectation
Lying down on the table
She opens her heart and soul
To receive the divine impetus
That moves through me
I am a resonant core
Connected
Present
Listening to the silence
Waiting instruction
She receives the vibration
Trusting
That what will be
Will be
Her body engages
Taps in
Takes over
It moves
And shifts
From dislocated chaos
To a new place
Of being

Amber Waters© 11/13/97

She has aligned
Her body
Her mind
Her spirit
Peacefully balanced
With where it needs to be
For the moment
She is my client
I am hers ❤

In love and respect
I am,
Amber Waters

For Randi. I honor you for being so receptive and taking responsibility for your own healing.

Amber Waters© 11/13/97

Mollye and Sammy
50th Anniversary

We say "hello" Mollye,
Oh, "hello" Sammy!
It's so nice to be here with you all.

You're looking swell Mollye,
Looking great Sammy!
It's so nifty that you've reached this fifty date.

So keep it up Sammy,
Give Mollye a whammy!
For it's never too late to celebrate.

So give a cheer to Sam and Mollye dear,
And let's all get together next year!

and "Mazel Tov". ❤

With Much Love,
Doris, Howard, Laurie and Carolyne

Aunt Mollye is Howard's Mom's sister, and their side of the family is very close. Doris' husband was a first cousin, so we all went to the party of Uncle Sam and Aunt Mollye. We love to find ways to get together, especially for happy occasions. This was a joint effort and may be sung to the song "Hello Dolly". "Mazel Tov" is a Jewish expression meaning lots of luck and good wishes.

Howard, Laurel and Carolyne Freeman and Doris Bardon© 11/2/91

Woman, Women

Woman, Women
Woman, Women
Women, Woman
Come together in community.

Bring your mind's eye open so you may learn
Open your eyes brightly to see
Open the windows of your ears to hear clearly
Take in a breath of life and
Smell all the odors around you.

Bring your voice and let it be heard.
Taste the foods that care for and nourish your body.
Bring your heart beating to
its own rhythm and rhyme, not mine.

You bring who you are and ! will bring me,
and we will celebrate,
and we will celebrate diversity.

Bring your sensuality and sexuality
therein every cell of your being.
You bring who you are and I will bring me,
and we will celebrate, and we will celebrate
a woman's community. ❤

Shirley is a long time friend, wife, mother,
thinker and a person who cares about the world. This is a song poem.

Shirley Kiser© Date Unkown

The Goddess

The goddess whispering love
Is like a moment of music.
Singing in the forest
The essential symphony of
Wind,
Moon,
and
Sun.
Sleeping
and
Dreaming
of
Bare feet in the garden. ❤

Paul is a friend and massage therapist who has joined us for many Thanksgiving gatherings.
This was one of his poems he shared.

Paul Henderson© Date Unknown

Brothers

I came to find the grave of my friend's brother.
Darkness filled in fast around the stones, and
Tears I brought to lay upon one special mark
Were shed upon three others resting there.
They were also someone's brother.

I was helpless in the twilight.
There seemed no exit from this
place without connecting to the loss.
The vacancy of life around those left here to cry.
To shake away the loss of just
one smiling face was futile.
The multitudes insured my fate.

I never found his spot before the dark.
But as the moon came up above them all,
I knew it was a moon that knows
no family lines,
no sides,
no blood.
It is a moon that chides us lest
we claim each fallen one as our own brother. ❤

Katherine Todd Smith is a long time friend and artist.
We have shared many ideas through the years.

Katherine Todd Smith© 11/11/92

To Val Cushing

Years before a letter came
requesting words
to celebrate your fame.
My eyes and hands did say
a reverent thank you
for your spirit shared so
easily at Alfred.

A graceful light adorns the face
of those who teach to learn,
and fills each vessel
richly in the burn.

When heart and light and heat do meet,
a star is born
not only in the kiln and sky.
You gave me this at Alfred. ❤

Class of 1972

---

*Katherine wrote this for one of her favorite art
instructors at college for a class reunion.*

Thoughts From Friends and Clients

"Let me puff myself up from the table." ❤
Diane, 10/87

"My muscles just fainted." ❤
Helen Andersen, 1/24/96

"Massage is an oasis in my day." ❤
D.J. Head, 6/1/99

"When we stop growing, we start dying." ❤
John Cox, 4/97

"Don't worry about the mule going blind,
just load the wagon." ❤
Big Ern, 6/1/99

"I didn't know this would be so much fun." ❤
Jim Utley, 4/19/99

"We are where we are because that is
really where we want to be." ❤
Ben Campen, Date Unknown

Time

When time unfolds a hoary web
To grasp, to hold, to keep
When time this web does further thread
Then do mortals weep.

The years roll in one by one
Treasured memories there,
their ways do wend
For whatever life from womb hath sprung
There its narrowed path doth end. ❤

Morris Mitzner celebrated his 85th birthday on June 1, 1999. He is a kind and loving person.
Morris is the husband of my 2nd cousin, Henrietta, who is having her 80th birthday this year.
This poem was written several years ago.

Morris Mitzner© Date Unknown

When I Was a Lad

When I was a lad I felt that I was free
To engage in acts of juvenile delinquencee.
So I spent quite an inordinate amount of time
Appropriating objects from the Five and Dime.
Chorus: (Appropriating objects from the Five and Dime!)

I appropriated objects so relentlesslee
That now I'm busy doing psychotherapee!
Chorus: (He appropriated objects so relentlesslee
That now he's busy doing psychotherapee!)
Ooompah oompah oompah oom—

My life of crime filled me right up to the hilt
With almost incapacitating pangs of guilt.
That guilt stimulated me to start a search for knowledge
About the human psyche, so I went away to college.
Chorus:
(About the human psyhe, so he went away to college.)

I sought that psycho-knowledge so assiduouslee
That now I'm really doing psychotherapee!
Chorus: (He sought that psycho-knowledge so assiduoslee
That now he's really doing psychotherapee!)
Ooompah oompah oompah oom—

I bounced from school to school and
I jumped from job to job;
With people from all walks of life I managed to hob-nob.
I floundered and I stumbled as my dizzy self I hurled
Into the frantic maelstrom of this polyglottal world.

David Lane© June,1990

Chorus:
(Into the frantic maelstrom of this polyglottal world.)

I floundered and I stumbled with such unmitigated glee
That now I'm <u>happy</u> doing psychotherapee!
Chorus:
(He floundered and he stumbled
with such unmitigated glee
That now he's <u>happy</u> doing psychotherapee!)
<u>Ooo</u>mpah <u>oo</u>mpah <u>oo</u>mpah oom—

Now, dear fellow Elderhost'lers, if you want your progenee
To follow in my footsteps and fulfill their destinee,
If they're not afraid of taking risks and acting like a fool,
Advise them to be guided by this golden rule:
Chorus: (Advise them to be guided by this golden rule:)

"Devote yourselves to floundering and petty thieveree
And you <u>all</u> may be doing <u>PSYCHOTHERAPEE!!!</u>"
Chorus:
("Devote yourselves to floundering and petty thieveree
And you <u>all</u> may be doing <u>PSYCHOTHERAPEE!!!</u>")

Alternate last line:
(And you may all be <u>getting</u> psychotherapee!!!)

David Lane is now a retired psychotherapist. In 1990, he and his wife went to an
elderhostel workshop at Bridgewater College, Virginia. The topic was Gilbert and Sullivan,
with an emphasis on the <u>HMS Pinafore</u>. One of the options was to compose a poem
modelled on the "Ruler of the Queen's Navee!!" There were certain rules including
the number of lines, for all poems entered in the contest.
This was the winning poem. One may sing or recite "When I Was a Lad".
Also optional, it may be sung by a psychotherapist, to add more meaning.

David Lane© June,1990

First Thoughts of Massage

First Version

When I get a massage
from Laurie Freeman
I feel so fine!
It's a wonderful kind of
Wide-awake dreamin'
I'm on Cloud Nine... ❤

The Ego-less Version

when   get a massage
from laurie freeman
feel just fine!
a wonderful kind of
wide-awake dreamin'
on cloud nine... ❤

*David Lane was one of my first long term clients. He wrote several poems for me early
on in our client/therapist relationship. David has his Ph.D in psychology and
recently retired after over 40 years of helping people.*

David Lane© 7/29/88

...Second Thoughts

When Laurie wants me to lie prone.
I do so with a happy moan.
And when she says to lie supine.
I float away upon cloud nine.
Whether I'm prone or I'm supine,
I joyfully groan --
"This feels divine!" ❤

I'm never sorry,
When I go to see Laurie.
I'm one of her fans.
It may sound nutty,
But I love to be putty
In her Hands. ❤

These poems make me giggle and hang on my office wall.
David Lane© 4/11/89 and 7/6/89

A Nifty Fifty

We're here together to celebrate
A very special Birthday date.

Five decades ago in the month of September
Occured an event, I well remember!

Nine months of waiting.....It felt like ten
The waiting ended.....And there was Ken.

Where would you be, If it weren't for me?
And your father, Indeed, who planted the seed?

It's hard to believe that we did conceive
In a moment of passion, a man child so dashin'!

A man of talents known far and wide
To family and friends, a source of pride.

A Lucky man in family and wife
He's sure to have a happy long life.

To sum it up.....I think it's nifty
That Ken has reached the age of fifty! ❤
Love,
Mother

Doris Bardon© 9/14/92

I Ache for You

Here for my massage today
Laurie smiled my fears away
and I thought it was OK
it did not turn out that way

As my muscles turned on bone
I released a startled groan
that became a constant moan
I'd been kneaded with a stone
With every move I would strain
my composure to maintain
but I struggled all in vain
she called it therapeutic pain

Her strong hands are gentle too
but I'm happy when she's through
Laurie, Laurie, yes it's true
my whole body aches for you. ❤

Larry Puckett © February, 1996

A Fragile Rose

When winter winds caress the
Rose
and bid each petal take
repose
the fragrance and the colors
dim
the Rose surrenders root and
stem

Then beauty's gone, save memories
kept
and petals fall where God has
stepped
A fragile Rose of gentle
grace
has left this world a better
place ❤

Insight

"Even
when
people
are
gone,

they
are
always
in
your
heart." ❤

Scottie Spurrier© Age 7, 1994

I Would Do Anything to Save You

For My Precious Mason

"Son of May,
from Far Away"
He came to earth,
first day of May
To sprinkle stars along his way.
He brought laughter and compassion
For that was also part of his mission.

And though just a boy
His wisdom was ancient.
His courage and true love
Will long be remembered
As to the Lord's hands his soul he surrendered.

And when one day he must go away
The many hearts that he humbled
Will break so wide open
We'll feel the earth tremble.

Dear son of May—
How I wish you could. ❤

Mason was a hospital friend of our daughter, Bonnie's. Although Mason was younger, they had many good times together, and they always had a smile on their face. Mason's Mom, Vivian Whitman, also known as Miz Viv, is a wonderful, compassionate woman. Only another Mom can really know what takes place when a child is ill with cancer. There are no words to describe what happens. Love is all there is, and Miz Viv is a love child.

Vivian Whitman © December, 1987

Thanksgiving in Gainesville

Some things I love this time of year with ya 'll
The leaves turning yellow, before they fall

The autumn light
an egret in flight
the Gators winning
students grinning
the downtown fair
paintings by Ellie Blair
movies at the Hippodrome
basketball at the O'Dome
politics as usual
serious and casual
bookstores a million
mosquitoes a zillion

An early azalea heralding flowers to come
In green city where winter is minimum
Where cosy fires are not necessary but nice
and before distant jingle bells raise shopping price
we have reasons for our joy to be living
with Laurie, Howard and Carolyne's Thanksgiving
For today we celebrate a simple wish
Love to all and a turkey on the dish ❤

Ian and Sara are dear friends who join us for the Thanksgiving gathering.

Ian Phillips© November, 1998

Earth and Moon

Once the Earth and the Moon were lovers-always close
But the Earth would look at the stars and wonder
'Till the Moon looked up from their embrace.
She saw the twinkling promises and drifted yonder
Soon Earth and Moon were lovers no longer.

The Earth turned his back on the Moon
And she became a creature of the night
Chasing the pattern of stars in the sky
But forever in his sight
Her pale beauty still directed at the Earth.

Now he looks at her longingly
And dreams they will be together one day
He follows her every evening 'till dawn
But he knows she will not stay
Wordless at morning light she simply fades away.

Sometimes I think we are like the Earth and Moon
Forever revolving around each other
Always near but never again as close as one
The light that once was warm is cool
And when I reach out you are gone. ❤

Another Thanksgiving gathering.

Ian Phillips© November, 1997.

Heart

"When there is righteousness in the heart,
There is beauty in the character.
When there is beauty in the character,
There is harmony in the home.
When there is harmony in the home,
There is order in the nation.
When there is order in the nation,
There is peace in the world."♥

Sai Baba, Date Unknown

Soul

If there is light in the soul
There will be beauty in the person
If there is beauty in the person
There will be harmony in the house
If there is harmony in the house
There will be order in the nation
If there is order in the nation
There will be peace in the world. ♥

Chinese Proverb, Date Unknown

If all the people in the world thought with their heart and soul for peace.
We would have peace.

The Journey

Do you
know
where
you
are
on
your
journey? ❤

Pathways on a Journey
Book Order Form

We are all on a journey. The paths we choose shape us into who we are. Our environment also helps shape us. Who we ultimately become is directly related to our chosen attitude. This book of poetry and thoughts is a journey depicting many paths. When ordering this book, please know at least $1 dollar from every book sold will go to charities. If you are interested in using *Pathways on a Journey* as a fund raiser, please contact the author.

To order, fill out the form below and mail with your check payable to:

Freeman USA, Inc.
2622 NW 43rd Street Ste C1
Gainesville, FL 32606
♦ [352] 371-9689 ♦ email: ljf@gdn.net ♦

# of Books	Price [includes 6%Florida Tax]
1 - 4	$10.00 each
5 - 9	$ 9.50 each
10 +	$ 9.00 each

Please allow 6 to 8 weeks for delivery. U.S. mail shipping and handling $3.^{00} for 1st book; each additional book $1.^{00}.

✍ **Please Print and Return or Copy and Return** ✍

Name: _____

Address: _____

City: _____

State: _____ Zip: _____

Phone: _____

# of Books x Price = Total Amt of Purchase:

_____ x _____ = _____

Shipping (if applicable): _____

AMOUNT ENCLOSED: _____